D1431423

Teaching Kids to Care

REFLECTIONS, ACTIVITIES & PRAYERS ON PRACTICING VIRTUES

Sr. Janet Schaeffler, OP

**TWENTY-THIRD
PUBLICATIONS**
twentythirdpublications.com

TWENTY-THIRD PUBLICATIONS
One Montauk Avenue, Suite 200
New London, CT 06320
(860) 437-3012 or (800) 321-0411
www.twentythirdpublications.com

Cover Photo: ©iStockphoto.com/timsa

ISBN: 978-1-62785-252-4
Library of Congress Control Number: 2016960017
Printed in the U.S.A.

A Division of Bayard, Inc.

CONTENTS

Introduction 4

Compassion 6

Consideration 9

Courtesy 12

Empathy 15

Forgiveness 18

Fortitude 21

Generosity 24

Gentleness 27

Gratitude 30

Helpfulness 33

Honesty 36

Humility 39

Integrity 42

Joyfulness 45

Justice 48

Kindness 51

Mercy 54

Patience 57

Peacefulness 60

Prudence 63

Respect 66

Responsibility 69

Simplicity 72

Trustworthiness 75

Wonder 78

INTRODUCTION

There are numerous books, articles, social media posts, and videos today that give "the ultimate advice" on how to be happy, how to have successful lives.

In reality, we have known the answer for centuries: the virtues and characteristics of living a life of care for others result in our happiness and success, but also go much further. They make a difference in the lives of others and make the world a better place—a beginning of the reign of God.

At times, today's culture exhibits bullying, lines of separation, a me-first attitude, and other self-centered behaviors. More than ever, we are called to live—and to pass on to our children—the gospel way of living: "This is my commandment, that you love one another as I have loved you" (John 15:12).

This booklet explores some of the key virtues/characteristics that are second nature for a person who follows Jesus. In reality, these virtues (and the many others) are interconnected. One builds on another; one reinforces another (e.g., if we are empathetic, we will also be considerate).

We will look at several approaches and activities for each of the virtues (to use at home and in the faith-formation setting). But three of the approaches that are not included in the following pages are primary, and they apply to all the virtues.

First, research and all human behavior illustrate that we learn best not from words, but through example. Our actions speak louder than words. If we desire to nurture certain traits within our children/youth, we must first develop those traits in ourselves. "Do as I say, not as I do" simply does not work, particularly when it comes to teaching the human values of caring. The best way to pray (and live) is to first become what we're praying for the other person to be.

Second, as catechists, teachers, and parents, we sometimes call attention to children's unsuitable behavior. That is, of course, necessary. At the same time, do we spend as much (or more) time in "catching them" in all the good things they're already doing? How do we point out—and stress—all the instances of gospel living already happening in the world around us?

Third, as important as it is to have, perhaps, one session/one unit on each specific virtue, our young people will absorb and grow into them when they're woven into everything that we do, when children/youth can witness them, talk about them, and have ways to practice them continually in everyday life.

May you experience God's blessings and strength around you as you live, teach, and lead others in living the best of being human, in living how God created us: to be people of compassionate caring and vibrant virtue.

1

Compassion

*The quality of being aware of and understanding the suffering
of others and wanting to do something about it*

REFLECTION FOR CATECHISTS

Regarded as one of the greatest virtues by all religions, compassion enables us to connect to human suffering with caring understanding, acting to bring comfort to those around us. "Compassion" says Pope Francis, "is a most profound word: compassion means 'to suffer-with-another.'" Speaking about Jesus healing a leper in the gospels, Pope Francis says: "Jesus' heart manifests God's paternal compassion for [the leper],...moving close to him and touching him. And this detail is very important." Pope Francis echoes St. Peter Claver's thought: "We must speak to them with our hands, before we try to speak to them with our lips."

APPROACHES

- Begin a Kids Care Club
  (*http://www.kidscare.org/kids-care-clubs*).

- Help your learners make a compassionate difference in the world through organizations such as Kids Can Make a

Difference (*www.kidscanmakeadifference.org*), Free the
Children (*www.freethechildren.org*), Roots and Shoots (*www.
janegoodall.org*), or Peace Jam, in which students work
directly with Nobel Peace Laureates (*www.peacejam.org*).

ACTIVITIES

• Ask: Who are three people you recognize as
compassionate? What do they do that makes them
compassionate?

• Make service experiences joyous. Sometimes witnessing
the reality can become depressing. The motto of the Little
Brothers of the Poor is "bread and flowers." They
recognize the whole person when they visit the elderly
poor. They realize that "necessities" go beyond basic food
and shelter and also include nourishment for the human
spirit.

• Help your learners reflect on times they have served/been
compassionate. What happened to them? Where did they
meet Jesus?

• Use children's books that help children understand the
experiences of others: *My Secret Bully, The Invisible Boy,
The Friendship Puzzle, My Brother Charlie, The Hundred
Dresses, Horace and Morris but Mostly Dolores*.

• Pray with current events. Invite youth to go through
newspapers/internet news to find people/groups in need
of prayer and compassion. Invite them to write a short
prayer for these, asking God's help and pledging their own
action.

- Involve your children when you give money to charities, help a sick relative, give clothes to the homeless, or take a neighbor who doesn't drive to the supermarket.

- Connect a real face to compassion: take turns during the week phoning or Skyping with a lonely person to share a friendly hello and to listen for a few minutes; visit a nursing home on a regular basis—visit the same person (perhaps someone who doesn't get any visitors) or a few people to establish a relationship with them.

PRAYER

God of compassion, open our eyes. Let us see those who are in need of compassion. Compel us to listen and to hear their needs. Give us hearts to be interested and hands to compassionately care.

2

Consideration

To have regard or respect for; a desire to avoid doing something that will make another person sad, upset, or angry

REFLECTION FOR CATECHISTS

Consideration might be said to be the basis of all living—certainly for all living as a follower of Jesus! Marian Wright Edelman, a strong advocate for acting with consideration, said, "Being considerate of others will take you and your children further in life than any college or professional degree." Being considerate comes in many shapes and sizes; opportunities abound in our everyday lives. St. Paul reminds us, "Let love be sincere...love one another with mutual affection; anticipate one another in showing honor" (Romans 12:9a, 10).

APPROACHES

- Help your learners be more considerate by learning to read the body language of others. For instance, a frown could indicate that someone could use a smile; a sharp tone could indicate that someone is frustrated. Help them realize that body language is an opportunity to offer consideration.

- Encourage your learners to pay attention to people whom they might easily dismiss (e.g., the new child in the group, service workers, etc.).

ACTIVITIES

- Brainstorm ways to be considerate: holding the door open for others, saying thank you to store clerks, giving the largest piece of candy to a friend, etc.

- Go on a photo scavenger hunt. Ask children to take pictures of examples of consideration.

- Research the saints to find out how they showed consideration—St. Francis of Assisi, St. Elizabeth Ann Seton, St. Bridget of Sweden, Venerable Catherine McAuley, Venerable Pierre Toussaint, Venerable Solanus Casey, and more.

- Make bookmarks that support a specific theme—such as saving the environment or protecting endangered species—to help them learn that consideration includes being kind to animals and the environment. Research and include facts on the bookmarks. Ask the local librarian if your group can donate the bookmarks so others can use them when they check out books.

SUGGESTIONS FOR FAMILIES

- Include your children in problem-solving situations that have led to past trouble. For example, children in the car: one wants to listen to the radio; one wants to sing aloud; another wants the others to be quiet. Before venturing out again, ask for suggestions on how they can show consideration for one another. Their solutions might surprise you!

- Have a goal that each family member will do (at least) two considerate things each day. Share your actions at dinner or bedtime.

PRAYER

O God, circle us with your love. Remind us to be a circle of consideration that continually reaches out to others. We give thanks that your love—above us, beneath us, behind us, before us, within and around us—strengthens us to be considerate of all in your family.

3

Courtesy

Polite, considerate behavior that shows
respect for other people

Courtesy is the everyday ways we respect other people and enable social relations. In reality, courtesy contributes to the moral fabric of our shared lives. Courtesy is an attitude of the heart that is self-giving. "Finally, be all like-minded, compassionate, loving, tenderhearted, courteous" (1 Peter 3:8).

APPROACHES

- Help young people reflect on why courtesy matters. Help them to appreciate that courtesy is also a form of empathy. Practicing courtesy gives children a deeper appreciation of and respect for themselves and others. Everything that we do has an impact on others.

- Courtesy manifests itself in manners. Look for all the ways and instances in which you can compliment and encourage your youngsters in their thoughtful manners toward you and one another.

- The increasing use of technology in our everyday lives has created a whole new reason for teaching manners; be sure frequently to help children to practice courtesy on the web, on the phone, and in social media.

ACTIVITIES

- Invite youngsters to compile an alphabet of courtesy; e.g., E: Elbows off the table; M: Magic words—please and thank you; T: Thank always.

- Brainstorm a list of courtesies that each child/youth agrees to for the strengthening of your learning community, e.g., not interrupting when someone else is talking, greeting people by name, saying "excuse me" or "pardon me," etc. This discussion could pave the way for setting rules for your group.

- Use books, such as: *Goops and How to Be Them; Be Polite and Kind; Are You Quite Polite?: Silly Dilly Manners Songs; Dude, That's Rude!: (Get Some Manners); 365 Manners Kids Should Know: Games, Activities, and Other Fun Ways to Help Children and Teens Learn Etiquette.*

- Invite your learners to design—and produce—commercials about everyday courtesy.

- Make a list of things courteous people say, such as: "Please"; "Thank you"; "I appreciate that"; "May I hold the door?"; "Pardon me"; and "I'm sorry I offended you."

- Provide your children with various experiences. Teach them how to behave at a concert, at a play, in a museum, in a restaurant, etc.

- During various everyday activities, suggest the courteous way of responding. For example: helping someone with a heavy bag of groceries, opening the door for others, thanking the store clerk, writing thank-you notes, using an inside voice when indoors, caring for borrowed possessions, asking people how they are, knocking on closed doors instead of just barging in, and never making fun of anyone.

PRAYER

*God of kindness and consideration, we bring your love
to our world when we act as you would, when we act as Jesus did.
Help us to see you in each person, treating them
with compassion, courtesy, and consideration.*

4

Empathy

The ability to understand and enter into the feelings, needs, and experiences of others

"Amid a culture of indifference...our style of life should instead be devout, filled with empathy, compassion and mercy" (Pope Francis, 2015). Empathetic people understand what others are feeling; they look at things from their perspective, wishing to relieve their pain and help to better the situation.

APPROACHES

- Encourage children/youth to develop empathy for one new person or group of people. Who is one person (group) that we might think of as "them"? What might be their struggles, their hopes, their similarity to us?

- Encourage your learners to build empathy: whenever they begin to make a judgment about someone (negative or positive), add the phrase "just like me." For example, "she is so selfish, just like me"; "he is so generous, just like me."

- When you are aware of people being bullied or hurt in movies, television, or books, begin a conversation about how these people must feel. Ask your learners how they would feel in that situation and what they would do to make it better. Point out ways characters helped out, or didn't, and have them think up different ways to help.

- Sometimes collecting food or clothes, etc., can separate us from the reality of the person in need. Have the organizations you are collecting for give you some profiles to share with your learners. If possible, have volunteers come and share these stories themselves.

- Refer to a world map when something happens that children are aware of—one little step to making it a real place.

SUGGESTIONS FOR FAMILIES

- Take your children to a park in another area of your community. Meeting new people increases understanding and fosters empathy.

- Empathetic children are not only conscious of others' feelings; they can also see themselves as capable of doing something to alleviate others' suffering. Praise your child when he or she shows concern for another. Point out their friends' feelings and suggest how they could help in some way. For instance, "Look at Abby's face. See how sad she is? Can you think of anything that would help her feel better?"

God of all, sometimes I want to be with people who look like me, act like me, and think like me. Yet you've created us as one family, one remarkable family with many differences. You call us to live in community. Deepen our empathy, our ways of feeling with others, of understanding each one and appreciating the beauty of all. May your empathy lead us to more and more feel your presence with us.

5

Forgiveness

Letting go of the desire to get even with someone;
to stop feeling anger toward someone/about something

REFLECTION FOR CATECHISTS

In everything we pray, in all Jesus teaches us, we know that God forgives us because we have, first, forgiven others. "This outpouring of mercy cannot penetrate our hearts as long as we have not forgiven those who have trespassed against us..." (***Catechism of the Catholic Church***, 2840).

APPROACHES

- Help children understand the steps of forgiveness: acknowledging what happened, experiencing feelings, asking God's help, forgiving, letting it go.

- Help children to realize that forgiving is something *we* do. The other person doesn't need to do anything, and he or she doesn't owe you a favor in return. In fact, the other person might not even be sorry.

ACTIVITIES

- Include prayers of forgiveness in prayer times; celebrate prayer services of reconciliation.

- Invite children to work in small groups to create a poem, a song, a rap, or a chant about forgiveness. Their words can tell why forgiveness is important and how it could make the world a better place.

- Create rituals to celebrate forgiveness. For example, write the event down, then rip the paper up, soak the pieces in water, squeeze them into a tiny ball, and bury it in the garden.

- Write a commercial about forgiveness. Try to sell forgiveness so others will begin to make it a way of life. For instance, say something positive that might happen in the world if more people forgave one another.

- During the summer, email your families inviting them to celebrate global forgiveness day (July 7): *http://www.ceca. cc/global_forgiveness_day/*

SUGGESTIONS FOR FAMILIES

- Help your children explore the reality that sometimes we need to look beyond the action and to seek to understand the person and what might have precipitated their actions. For example, if your child is upset because Timmy called him a name during recess, guide your child to ask what was happening (Timmy had just been excluded from a game; he was jealous of those who were chosen; etc.).

- During dinner or in the car, talk about forgiveness: When have you been forgiven? How do you know you've been forgiven? Why do you think the person forgave you? Do you think the person you hurt felt better or worse after they forgave you? How did you feel after you were forgiven? What is your relationship like with the person now? Did this experience make you more or less likely to repeat the hurtful behavior?

PRAYER

Forgiving God, your love and forgiveness are always there for us. Help me to let go of hurts; help me to forgive others. Help me to let go of anger and grudges; help me to reach out in loving care to others.

6

Fortitude

*The strength and courage that allows someone to encounter
and endure the challenges of life, the pain, danger, or adversity
no matter what the cost*

REFLECTION FOR CATECHISTS

Fortitude, a gift of the Holy Spirit and a cardinal virtue, is sometimes called courage, but goes deeper. "Fortitude is the moral virtue that ensures firmness in difficulties and constancy in the pursuit of the good. It strengthens the resolve to resist temptations and to overcome obstacles in the moral life. The virtue of fortitude enables one to conquer fear, even fear of death, and to face trials and persecutions" (***Catechism of the Catholic Church***, 1808). Fortitude is the power to do what is right, even when difficult. It allows us to face every difficulty with inner peace and courage. Fortitude allows us to carry out our duties, even if doing so might require great sacrifice and suffering.

APPROACHES

- Help children explore examples of fortitude: facing physical pain when necessary (tiredness, lack of sleep, cold, heat, hunger, injuries, etc.); facing disapproval or ridicule when doing the right thing; being willing to be different from other people, when necessary.

- Help children learn that they should face difficulties and pain and not run from them. They should not be surprised by difficulties and pain and should understand that they are part of life. Help them learn how to discern what difficulties they should face and which they should not face, and how to size up difficulties realistically.

ACTIVITIES

- Invite learners to read one of the following Scripture passages, choosing a word or phrase that stands out for them: Daniel 3:13–24; Psalm 23; Psalm 42:5–6; Psalm 43:2–5; Psalm 91; Mark 10:46–52; Matthew 26:36–46; Luke 11:5–13; Luke 18:1–8.

- Invite youngsters to research examples of fortitude: in Scripture (Abraham, John the Baptist, Paul); in history (St. Francis Xavier, Sts. Perpetua and Felicity, St. Monica, Dietrich Bonhoeffer, Martin Luther King Jr., Rosa Parks, Alexander Solzhenitsyn), and in our own day.

- Create trading cards illustrating people of fortitude, writing a prayer on one side of the card.

- Give encouragement. When your children are going through tough times, encourage them, counsel them, and help whenever necessary. Let them know you are there when they need you. Pray for them and enlist the prayers of others for them.

- Discuss with your children a time when you managed to get through a difficult situation because of courage/fortitude.

- As a family, memorize a Scripture passage that is based upon fortitude. For example: Exodus 15:2; Psalm 23:4; Psalm 27:13–14; Matthew 14:25–27; Hebrews 12:1.

PRAYER

God of courage, remind me always of the words in Joshua:
"Be strong and courageous! Do not fear or be dismayed,
for the Lord your God is with you wherever you go."
Guide my decisions and actions as I live the gift of fortitude.

7

Generosity

*The willingness to freely and unselfishly share who we are and what we
have with others, often providing more than is needed or normal*

REFLECTION FOR CATECHISTS

Generosity isn't about giving money (although at times that is
helpful/important). It's about the giving of ourselves. "Dear
young people, the Church expects great things of you and your
generosity. Don't be afraid to aim high" (Pope Francis; tweet,
October 16, 2015).

APPROACHES

- Reflect on generosity as a responsibility. Is it something
  we do above and beyond our everyday actions, or is it a
  normal part of our responsibility?

- While it's important to recognize generous behavior, be
  careful about rewarding it. Being generous is not about
  getting recognition. Saying "I'm proud of the way you
  participated in the parish's Giving Tree; imagine how it
  helped others," is more effective than saying "Good for
  you. We'll have a treat because you were generous."

- Invite guest speakers from various service organizations in your parish and civic community.

- Help children think about and research people in the community who need help—the elderly, the disabled, the poor. Explore ways they can be generous to those in hospitals, soup kitchens, etc.

- There are countless stories of children's magnificent generous acts. Invite your learners to watch for them, to do research and find them (e.g., *http:// littleredwagonfoundation.com/; http://www.coatsofkindness. org/; http://www.dailygood.org/view.php?sid=198; http:// blog.goinspirego.com/2012/10/boy-6-with-brain-cancer- brings.html; http://blog.goinspirego.com/2010/03/6-year- old-inspires-movement-feeds.html*). Reflect with them: Do these actions give you any ideas of what you might do? Of what we might do together as a group?

- Invite your learners to search Scripture, especially the Book of Proverbs, for passages/challenges about living generously.

- Encourage your learners to notice the gifts all around them and to think of people to share them with. For example, are their shelves at home filled with books? Suggest they donate some to a local family shelter.

- Involve your children in charitable giving decisions and in discussions about what you buy.

- Brainstorm with your children ways to help others while remaining anonymous. For example, anonymously leave a box of groceries on the doorstep of a widow/widower or single parent; color pictures and mail them, along with gift cards to grocery or department stores, to families in need; pay for registration for camps or workshops, sending a note telling the families so (without telling them who paid it).

- Establish a "family foundation." Create a homemade bank for donations. Parents, children, visitors, and friends can put money in the bank. Children can be introduced to tithing when they receive gifts, earnings, or allowance. Choose a charity together to give to—one that has an especially personal meaning for the children.

PRAYER

Lord, teach me to be generous. Teach me to give and not to count the cost. (ST. IGNATIUS)

8

Gentleness

*Having a kind and quiet nature; responding with sensitivity,
tenderness and compassion*

REFLECTION FOR CATECHISTS

Gentleness is a fruit of the Holy Spirit as well as the third
Beatitude. "By this power of the Spirit, God's children can bear
much fruit…'love, joy, peace, patience, kindness, goodness,
faithfulness, gentleness, self-control'" (*Catechism of the Catholic
Church*, 736).

Sometimes people think gentleness is weakness. It is the op-
posite: "Nothing is so strong as gentleness, nothing so gentle as
real strength" (St. Francis de Sales). Jesus teaches us gentleness;
he showed God's love with quiet strength. He was gentle with
people's hearts.

APPROACHES

- For prayer time, choose Scripture passages that speak of
  gentleness: Proverbs 15:1; Proverbs 16:24; Ephesians 4:2;
  Philippians 4:5; Colossians 3:12–14.

- Keep a chart entitled "Gentleness." Make a list of words that
  describe gentleness as you read different Scripture verses.

- Give each child an uncooked egg in a Ziploc bag to be carried around during the day—in their hands, in a pocket, etc., but they must not set it down. At the end of the day, check on the eggs. Explain that these eggs could be symbols of people's feelings. Gentleness means treating everyone with care, similar to "caring" for these eggs.

- For two weeks, invite your learners to keep a journal of how they have lived the third Beatitude. (This activity could be continued with the other Beatitudes.)

- A classic book, *Fuzzies: A Folk Fable for All Ages*, speaks about gentleness (warm fuzzies) (*http://www. claudesteiner.com/fuzzy.htm; http://www.holycomforter.org/ fuzziesandpricklies/*). Go outside, looking for warm fuzzies and cold pricklies in nature. After bringing them inside, decide what kind of words or actions would go along with each object: gentle and kind, or cruel and harsh. The objects can be put into a bowl, serving as a reminder of our call to be gentle in all we do.

- Using a month-long calendar, each evening help your children think of one thing they did that demonstrated gentleness, writing it on the calendar. You could also talk about gentle ways at the beginning of the month, writing each on a slip of paper, placing them in a jar. Have your children pull a slip from the jar each day and try to do what is written on it before the end of the day.

- Various studies remind us that children tend to imitate behavior they see on television. You may want to limit their viewing of violent programs and encourage them to watch shows that promote gentle caring and helping.

PRAYER

Gentle God, guide me to be gentle in the things I say and do.
Show me new ways to be gentle to all I meet, in all I do.

9

Gratitude

The feeling and expression of being appreciative for gifts, for things that have happened (or not happened), for something or someone who exists

REFLECTION FOR CATECHISTS

Often we're bombarded by the media to be dissatisfied and to always want more. Within this culture, fostering gratitude can be our Christian response. "Gratitude is a flower that blooms in noble souls" (Pope Francis). Gratitude begins with an interior disposition and often tries to express itself in words and deeds. Thus, it includes three elements: acknowledgment of a gift that has been received, appreciation expressed in thankfulness, and, whenever possible, some return for what has been freely given with no obligation on the donor's part.

APPROACHES

- Leave a basket of thank-you notes on or near your prayer table as an invitation to write prayers of thanks, and to write notes of thanks to people.

- Work gratitude into your daily/weekly conversations (and your group prayer).

- Each week, invite your learners to concentrate on one category of things they're grateful for—small things, sweet things, people who help but whose names we don't know, gifts it's hard to say thank you for, etc.

- Invite your learners to write letters to the editor of your local community paper, highlighting and thanking someone who is a kind and caring neighbor.

- Paint a Grateful Tree on a wall in your meeting space or in the hallway; encourage your learners and visitors to write their thanks on the wall or on painted leaves, making a visual witness of gratitude to all who come and go.

- Make a Giving Thanks Jar. Decorate a jar, and beside it have little pieces of paper ready to write on. At times, specifically invite children to write about something they are grateful for; encourage them also to add other notes whenever they wish. Periodically, open the jar and incorporate the many thank yous into your group's prayer.

SUGGESTIONS FOR FAMILIES

- Keep an ongoing family gratitude list on the refrigerator or leave a family gratitude journal open on a table, inviting frequent additions.

- Once a week, have a family thank-you note writing time. Gather together to write thank-you notes, individually or one as a family, to someone who touched your lives the past week (think, too, of the unsung people in your lives).

- Tune in to simple things. Turn off all technology, go outside, and appreciate and be grateful for the simple beauty of a sunrise, the falling rain, or the many things we can usually take for granted.

PRAYER

God of all gifts, thank you! You have given me more than I could ever imagine. Nudge me to give thanks to all the people you have given me—those I know and those who might touch my life for only a moment.

10

Helpfulness

Making it easier to do a job, deal with a problem, etc.;
providing service or assistance

Even though some people will say that children are selfish, if we just watch, we will often see that they are naturally sympathetic and have a desire to be helpful. Parents, teachers, and caring adults who surround them can build on this, helping them to grow up with a sense of selfless giving without always expecting something in return. We are called to a broad sense of this selfless giving: "We have to become courageous Christians and seek out those [who need help most]"(Pope Francis, May 18, 2013).

APPROACHES

- Help children/youth understand that helping is requested and required "just because"—just because they're members of this learning community. Decide on ways to help make your time/space an enjoyable and safe place. Invite them to take turns helping in various ways.

- Often we think of ways to be helpful over the holidays.

Create an atmosphere of continual helping so that children will realize that a generous heart is important all year round.

- Invite children to write ways to help their family (e.g., do someone else's chore; clean the kitchen). Make copies for each child; have each child decorate a shoe box, placing the various ideas inside. Have them take the boxes home; each morning, each family member chooses one idea, using it to help that day.

- It can seem that bad news surrounds us. Point out the good things that happen and the people who are helping others. Invite your group to bring newspaper/internet articles about groups or individuals, especially youth, who are making the world a better place.

- Have periodic discussions (or create role-plays) about ways children/families can help to lighten someone's load (e.g., meeting the mail carrier on the sidewalk before he or she walks up the drive or letting someone with fewer things go ahead in line at the supermarket).

- Have a family meeting to discuss what it means to be a family. Guide the discussion to include ways that family members help each other.

- Watch out for your neighbors. Is someone sick, struggling, grieving, or needing help?

- In addition to asking your children what they want for Christmas or other holidays, ask instead, "What do you want to give?" Help them explore ideas of what they can give to grandparents, sisters, brothers, or the other parent—something they can make or can afford to purchase. Talk about how simple things make great gifts.

PRAYER

Generous God, you give and give. I pray for a heart like yours, a giving and helpful heart. Show me how to make someone's day or to help them in a way that only I can. Make me sensitive to people's needs; open my hands.

11

Honesty

Speaking the truth and acting fairly and truthfully;
worthy of being depended upon

REFLECTION FOR CATECHISTS

St. Paul reminds us: "Let each one of you speak the truth to our neighbors, for we are members one of another" (Ephesians 4:25). In reality, honesty is more than words. It is who we are and how we act: keeping promises, being trustworthy, and taking responsibility for our choices.

APPROACHES

- Every chance you get, talk about how important "the truth" is. Don't wait for the middle of a situation. Comment on some of the broad realities of honesty (e.g., truth in advertising and the news, how truth keeps life simple, how the truth always comes out in the end).

- Talk about how truthful people are respected. Have a look at honesty themes in literature, such as *The Boy who Cried Wolf.*

- Explore honesty with questions such as:

  How many lies do you get to tell before you are a liar?

  What would you do if you found $500 and nobody saw you find it?

  Is it ok to tell a "small" lie to keep from upsetting someone?

  When people are dishonest with you, how does it make you feel?

  If your classmates are cheating on a test, does that make it right for you to do it also?

  Are there risks involved in being honest? In being dishonest?

- As a class, brainstorm the excuses and rationalizations people give for lying, cheating, and stealing. What might be wrong with each of them?

- Invite your learners to keep an honesty journal. Document examples of honesty and dishonesty in everyday life. Pay attention to ads, news, TV shows, etc. Is dishonesty ever at the core of these? At the end of a few weeks, analyze what they have discovered about everyday honesty.

- Conduct a survey in your neighborhood: Do you think people are honest enough? What types of honesty do you appreciate? What are some examples of dishonesty you really dislike? Compile the results into a news report to be shared with other classes.

- Children are bound to make mistakes. They might break a treasured dish or fail a test. Children might be fearful of parents' reactions, which then encourages lying to avoid anger or punishment. Create a safe home that will support a child to choose honesty. Behavior shouldn't go unnoticed; explain the consequences of actions while always respecting the person.

- Lying is usually a result; help your children to expand their awareness (which can lead to a change in behavior) by exploring the cause. Why did they lie?

PRAYER

Jesus, your words, your actions, your life were honest and true. We ask—because your strengthening presence surrounds us always—that we may follow your way, living lives of truth, honesty, and integrity.

12

Humility

The quality of an unassuming attitude, of not thinking you are better than other people

REFLECTION FOR CATECHISTS

Humility can be misunderstood. It is not weakness or disparaging ourselves; in reality, it is an appropriate thinking about ourselves—understanding and seeing ourselves as God sees us—and how God sees everyone. Humility enables us to place others first, to listen, to be courteous, because each and every one is unique—and loved by God. C.S. Lewis said, "Humility is not thinking less of yourself, but thinking of yourself less." Pope Francis suggested this could be our prayer—"Jesus, I want to be humble like you, humble like God."

APPROACHES

- Always help children/youth feel good about themselves. This may seem contradictory, but humility comes from a position of strength and self-assurance. Encourage them to be the very best they can be—no matter what they do.

- Help them to understand where their value comes from—from God, from their dignity as a loved creation of God (rather than from how smart or attractive or rich they might be).

- The essence of humility is the willingness to be one with others. Activities that involve cooperation can foster this. Reflect on the activities you invite children to be involved in: Do they promote cooperation or competition?

ACTIVITIES

- The best example of humility, of course, is seen in the life of Jesus. Invite your learners to search the gospels for examples of Jesus' humility.

- Invite them to think about people who are humble. For example, hockey player Steve Yzerman, captain of the Detroit Red Wings, always attributed his success to his coach and the players around him, not himself. He never called himself one of the "greats" even though he is a member of the NHL Hall of Fame.

- Invite reflection on the following Scripture passages. What would be humble thoughts and resulting actions flowing from them (e.g.: 1 Corinthians 10:24—we need to be willing to let others go first): Acts 20:35b; James 5:16a; Colossians 3:13–14; Psalm 133:1; Romans 12:18; Proverbs 1:7; Proverbs 19:20; Philippians 2:3; Ephesians 4:2)?

- Help your children to take satisfaction rather than pride in their accomplishments. When children perform well or achieve a goal, it's good for them to feel the joy that comes from a job well done, but arrogant or disrespectful behavior is not permitted.

- Encourage your children to admit mistakes. Help them realize that people think more of them, not less, when they admit mistakes. Help them consider the merits of suggestions/criticisms instead of instantly defending themselves.

PRAYER

Humble God, help us to learn humility: to praise, not criticize; to see the best in others; to learn from mistakes; to ask for help; to build, not destroy.

13

Integrity

*Having strong moral principles: choosing courage over comfort;
choosing what's right over what's easy; practicing values,
not simply professing them*

REFLECTION FOR CATECHISTS

"The Gospel calls individual Christians to live lives of honesty, integrity and concern for the common good. But it also calls Christian communities to create 'circles of integrity'...to transform society" (Pope Francis' homily in Manila, January 16, 2015).

C.S. Lewis once said, "Integrity is doing the right thing, even when no one is watching." Integrity is not a single action but a mind-set that influences our whole character. It comes from knowing who we are and whose we are.

APPROACHES

- Frequently provide good examples and bad examples of living in integrity. Point out actual happenings as well as suggesting various possible scenarios.

- Teach tolerance. Children that grow up surrounded by tolerance learn to accept others as they are, realizing that there is a common bond that transcends any differences. Help them understand that prejudice or racism is not tolerated and that not everyone has to think in the same way that they do.

- Engage the youngsters in a conversation about times they have taken an upopular stand. What did they do? What was the outcome? How did they feel afterwards? What did they learn from the experience?

- Invite your learners to make a list of the principles they would never compromise. Have them select one and write a short story (real or imagined) describing a time they did something courageous by standing up for this principle.

- Encourage the young people to bring in some newspaper or internet articles about people the students think have integrity and people they think do not. Discuss: What distinguishes one from the other? Who gets more play in the media?

- In small groups, invite your learners to write a letter to someone in the news whose integrity has impressed them.

- Invite older learners to write their own eulogy, describing how they want to be remembered. Then write about what they will need to do in their life to be remembered the way they would like.

- Integrity is composed of many other significant virtues—patience, honesty, responsibility, dependability, accountability, caring, etc. Because of its all-encompassing nature, it can creep into various family conversations. Mention it often.

- Help your children end the day with reflections such as these: How did I live a life of integrity today? Were there times when I wasn't a person of integrity? Is there something I would do differently tomorrow?

PRAYER

God of all goodness, you call us to be our best selves,
in your image and likeness. Guide us so that our lives will be
testimonies of all good things to our world.

14

Joyfulness

Cheerfulness; calm delight; deep happiness

REFLECTION FOR CATECHISTS

A fruit of the Holy Spirit, joy sends us forth. "Joy is a pilgrim...
The Christian sings with joy, and walks, and carries this joy. It is
the gift that brings us to the virtue of magnanimity" (Pope
Francis, May 10, 2013). Joy, God's gift, makes us feel good; when
we feel good, we do good; when we do good, it reminds others of
what joy feels like, inspiring them to do the same.

APPROACHES

- Help children understand that joy goes further than
  happiness, existing even in hard times. Happiness is based
  on circumstances; joy comes from inner strength.
  Happiness can be very fleeting; joy is more stable: "We
  know that all things work for good for those who love
  God..." (Romans 8:28).

- "Enter the room with a smile" could be a group rule. Post
  this poem:

SMILING

Smiling is infectious; you catch it like the flu.
When someone smiled at me today, I started smiling too.
I passed around a corner and someone saw my grin.
When he smiled, I realized I had passed it on to him.
I thought about that smile and then I realized its worth.
A single smile, just like mine, could travel around the earth.
So if you feel a smile begin, don't leave it undetected.
Let's start an epidemic quick and get the world infected.

(AUTHOR UNKNOWN)

ACTIVITIES

- Have your learners search Pope Francis' Twitter account and *The Joy of the Gospel* for his thoughts on joy.

- Read the Letter to the Philippians, watching for mentions of joy or rejoicing. Find the many joyful statements in the Book of Psalms, which were often created amid difficult circumstances.

- Sprinkle some white glitter on white paper and some on black paper. Notice which shows up the best. Explore how joy sometimes shows up better during the dark times.

- Help children count their blessings. Appreciation for everything in our lives, rather than always desiring what we don't have, is a foundation for joy.

SUGGESTIONS FOR FAMILIES

- Have a Family No Complaining Day (or Week). Slip a rubber band or bracelet on one of your wrists; if you complain, move it to the other wrist. Challenge everyone to go the whole day without moving their wrist reminder.

- Talk with your children about going to school grumpy or in a good mood. Explore how they can use God's gift of joy to make a day good or bad just with their outlook. "This is the day the Lord has made, let us rejoice and be glad in it" (Psalm 118:24).

PRAYER

God of lavish joy, let all your messages of joy touch me today. Make me a messenger of joy, bringing your gladness to someone who needs to be delighted.

15

Justice

The upholding of what is fair and right;
respecting the rights of others and establishing harmony
in relationships

REFLECTION FOR CATECHISTS

Justice is the cardinal virtue most frequently praised in the sacred Scriptures. All the Ten Commandments are concerned with justice. "Justice is the moral virtue that consists in the constant and firm will to give their due to God and neighbor" (*Catechism of the Catholic Church*, no. 1807). Social justice promotes the view that everyone deserves to enjoy the same economic, political, and social rights, regardless of race, socioeconomic status, gender, or other characteristics.

APPROACHES

*   Teach the difference between the virtues of charity and justice. Charity responds to the immediate needs (a hungry person, etc.). Justice wants to eliminate the social conditions that cause those needs (unemployment, racism).

- Explore "fairness." Does fairness mean everyone gets the same amount, like an equal piece of a chocolate bar? Does fairness mean enforcing the rules for everyone, even if it means losing a game? How is fairness related to having respect for others? How is it related to honesty? To being reliable? To being a good citizen?

- Help your learners to listen and to research, helping them look at both sides of an issue.

ACTIVITIES

- Encourage your learners to be on the lookout for examples of social justice in the world around them. Create a current events bulletin board and encourage your students to bring in newspaper articles and clippings from magazines that pertain to social justice. In your class, discuss justice-related issues such as charging teens with cyberbullying. Bring in audio-visual resources to make your presentation more engaging to your students.

- Use ideas from *http://www.usccb.org/beliefs-and-teachings/who-we-teach/youth/social-justice-youth-group-activity.cfm*

- Invite children to read overviews, diaries, letters, biographies, and poetry written by survivors of prejudice (the handicapped, Native Americans, African Americans, Japanese Americans during World War II, etc.), and share their findings with the group.

- Help children experience injustice with an activity such as: one half of the group receives fancy paper, colorful markers, and well-working scissors; the other half receives scrap paper and pencils. After they have each created paper puppets, explore their feelings. Compare this to other—much larger—situations in our world.

SUGGESTIONS FOR FAMILIES

- Help everyone realize that every decision they make (even small ones) affects other people. Think of a few decisions that individual family members have made, and talk about how those decisions affected everyone else.

- As a family, decide to write a letter a month (or week) to local and national leaders about issues of justice (human rights, just policies for the poor and/or the disabled, the environment, etc.).

PRAYER

Holy and loving God, we come to you for guidance.
Enlarge our hearts. Deepen our understanding.
Give us your passionate love for all your people.

16

Kindness

The quality of being gentle and considerate

REFLECTION FOR CATECHISTS

In his Second Letter to the Corinthians, St. Paul reminds us of Jesus' life: "By the meekness and kindness of Christ, I appeal to you..." (2 Corinthians 10:1). In other passages he reminds us of our own call: "clothe yourselves with...kindness..." (Colossians 3:12). In Galatians 5:22–23, St. Paul identifies kindness as one of fruits of the Spirit. Jesus' statement that "whatsoever you do to others, you do for me" is a reminder of the power of our actions of kindness. The Corporal Works of Mercy and the Prayer of St. Francis give us concrete examples of the work of kindness.

In reality, we don't want to work at doing just "kind acts," but, rather to have kindness be our very nature.

APPROACHES

- Visit the Random Acts of Kindness Foundation (*https:// randomactsofkindness.org/*) for free educational and community ideas, guidance, and other resources.

- Bring a travel-size toothpaste to your session. Ask if anyone can squeeze the entire tube out and then put it back into the tube. Proceed to squeeze out the toothpaste onto a plate and show how it cannot be put back. Compare this to our words: once we say unkind words, we can't take them back. We can apologize but they're still out there and have hurt others.

ACTIVITIES

- In contrast to an attitude of "every person for themselves," many researchers today are finding evidence suggesting that humans are successful as a species because of our traits of nurturing, compassion, and kindness. They call it "survival of the kindest." Search online for their conclusions and ways that people and communities are accentuating kindness.

- Invite children/youth to write a portrait of "The Kindest Person I Know," including specific examples of this person's kindness.

- Create a display in the entrance of your building with hearts containing suggestions of what children can do to show kindness to others, such as:

  » Ask a student you have never played with to join you at recess.

  » Pick up litter wherever you see it.

  » Pray for someone. Write them a note—anonymously—to tell them someone has been praying for them.

  » With your friends, hang around a neighborhood store where people carry lots of bags. Offer to help—accepting no tips, of course.

- Explain kindness to your children as often as possible. If your child helps their sibling pick up their toys, do more than say "thank you." When you tell them that doing what they did without being asked was a kind thing to do, you give them a concrete example of what kindness looks like.

- As a family decide on specific days of the week to focus on kindness in different areas: kindness at home; kindness in our neighborhood; kindness to those we don't know, etc.

PRAYER

God of kindness, you have created each and every one of us, while totally loving and caring for each of us. Help us to be like you. Help us to respond to everyone with the kindness that we have learned from you. Amen.

17

Mercy

Compassionate kindness and steadfast love shown to others, especially toward people who are suffering or in distressing situations

REFLECTION FOR CATECHISTS

"Be merciful as God is merciful" (Luke 6:36). Because God is always forgiving, compassionate, and generous to us, we are called to be people of mercy to others. "Mercy: the fundamental law that dwells in the heart of every person who looks sincerely into the eyes of his brothers and sisters on the path of life" (Pope Francis, Announcement of the Extraordinary Jubilee of Mercy, #2).

APPROACHES

- Invite a reflection on the following: I wonder how many ways there are to show mercy? What if there was no word at all for hate, just words for mercy? What if there was a department of mercy in every state?

- According to the ***Oxford Dictionary***, the definition of mercy is "compassion or forgiveness shown toward someone whom it is within one's power to punish or harm." When situations of bullying, teasing, mocking, and tormenting occur, refer your learners to this definition, drawing contrasts and exploring other alternatives.

ACTIVITIES

- Have your learners design a bumper sticker about mercy. Include on the bumper sticker: the word "mercy," a slogan for why you should live it, and at least three words that describe it.

- Use this virtue of mercy to explore the many facets of the Corporal and Spiritual Works of Mercy.

- Invite your youngsters to translate the Works of Mercy into practical things they can do, e.g., "feed the hungry"— give up snacks one day a week and give that money to
  _____.

- Your learners are probably doing more Works of Mercy than they recognize. Invite them to make a list. Help them to reflect: Which practice is most frequent or difficult or fun or unusual?

- Have your youngsters work in teams to rewrite Matthew 25:34–40 with modern acts of mercy. For example, "I was new in your school and you asked me to sit with you during lunch in the cafeteria." "I had a terrible cold and you brought me chicken soup and chocolate chip cookies."

- As a family, work together on an action flowing from the Works of Mercy: volunteering at a soup kitchen, cleaning the grounds of a park, bringing cheer to children in the hospital, collecting food for your local food bank, volunteering at your parish with the social concerns projects, making sandwiches or volunteering services for Habitat for Humanity's workers, organizing a neighborhood block party for a cause, etc.

- Let your refrigerator door preach about mercy. (Put up newspaper or internet articles, pictures, etc.)

PRAYER

Praise the Lord, for he is good; for his mercy endures forever. Praise the God of gods; for his mercy endures forever! **(Psalm 136: 1–2)**

18

Patience

The ability to remain calm in a difficult situation or with a person; to keep a good attitude in delay, trouble, or suffering without getting upset or angry

REFLECTION FOR CATECHISTS

Pope Francis reminds us that we learn patience, first of all, from Jesus: "The Word of God entered with 'patience' in the moment of the Incarnation and thus unto death on the Cross. Patience and perseverance" (Sept. 20, 2014). One of the fruits of the Holy Spirit, patience teaches the importance of delaying gratification, a skill necessary for maturity. Patience can help foster the ability to think through and solve problems. The value of patience lies in its gift of inner calm and emotional strength.

APPROACHES

- Today's tech culture exposes children to instant gratification. Choose projects and activities that require time, patience, and working together.

- When situations happen within your setting, help children depersonalize the circumstance. Often what's

bothering us is not directed at us—a delay in the
schedule, for example, isn't done to specifically aggravate
us.

- Place some oyster shells on your prayer table to remind
  everyone that pearls are formed with patience.

ACTIVITIES

- Psalm 37:7 reminds us: "Be still before the Lord and wait
  patiently for God." Lead children in a prayer of
  meditation, which helps them to slow down.

- Choose something from nature to observe and record how
  it changes over a month or two; e.g., a tree in the spring or
  fall, the phases of the moon, a growing plant, snow
  melting, tadpoles hatching, etc. As the children watch the
  changes, help them understand that some things can't be
  rushed. God's timing—for many things—is wise; we need
  to learn how to enjoy the waiting.

- Search Scripture for passages on patience: e.g., Ephesians
  4:2; 1 Thessalonians 5:14; Luke 2:22–38.

SUGGESTIONS FOR FAMILIES

- Practice patience at mealtime (e.g., waiting until everyone
  has been served before beginning to eat; eating slowly,
  using silverware; waiting until everyone is finished their
  first helpings before having seconds; and waiting patiently
  for an item to be passed). Talk about how mealtime is
  more enjoyable when we show patience and use respectful
  manners.

- When your child responds with "gimme," acknowledge the wish ("You wish you could have that toy right now"). Have them add it to a "wish list" of presents he or she might receive at the next birthday or gift-giving holiday. The act of writing down (or drawing or cutting out a magazine picture) gives your child control and increases patience.

PRAYER

Patient God, often I find it difficult to wait. Nudge me gently to have a loving, patient heart: patient to wait—and work— for your dreams, patient with all the people and happenings of my day.

19

Peacefulness

Manifesting calmness and tranquility;
undisturbed by turmoil or disagreement

REFLECTION FOR CATECHISTS

As disciples of Jesus, our call is not just about "not hurting"; rather it is a call to vigorously work to bring about peace. "Seek peace and pursue it" (1 Peter 3:11). The church proclaims "the Gospel of peace…the new evangelization calls on every baptized person to be a peacemaker" (Pope Francis, *The Joy of the Gospel*, 239).

We are called to continually deepen our connection to Jesus, the Prince of Peace—to grow in inner peace, to discover our gifts, and to use them to be peacemakers wherever we are.

APPROACHES

- Connect all your explorations about peace with the Beatitude "Blessed are the peacemakers, for they will be called children of God."

- Hold children accountable. If children stand by and watch someone being bullied, make it clear that their behavior hurts the victim too.

- Invite children/youth to keep an Inventory of Peace. When/where do they most feel the lack of peace? When do they feel "in conflict"? Why? How could these conflicts be resolved with peace?

- Lead children in quiet prayer times, deepening the inner peace that God gives.

- Have your learners make creative posters about peace. Ask your neighborhood businesses and stores to display them.

- Help children learn about various witnesses for nonviolence and peace: Martin Luther King Jr., Mahatma Gandhi; Malala Yousafzai; Nelson Mandela, St. John Paul II, Desmond Tutu, among others.

- Invite children/youth to write or paint to describe:

    a day that is filled with only peace

    their wish for peace

    their image/symbol for peace

- Celebrate the International Day of Peace (September 21) with prayer and action: *(http://www.un.org/en/events/ peaceday/index.shtml)*.

- Encourage older youngsters to study a conflict-ridden area of the world, looking at it from two or more perspectives. Help them learn that every conflict has many layers, and that to build peace one must work respectfully with all sides.

- Have regular family meetings to make family decisions, talking about any conflicts. A shared approach to making decisions and plans and resolving conflicts is probably the most important single mechanism for promoting peace and cooperation in the home.

- Choose peaceful forms of entertainment. Pay close attention to the messages that come to your children about conflict, violence, and peace from television, movies, toys, games, music, and literature. Talk about messages that are divergent from peacemaking. Make a family decision that no "war/violent toys" will have a place in your home.

PRAYER

Spirit of God, lead us from death to life, from falsehood to truth. Lead us from despair to hope, from fear to trust. Lead us from hate to love, from war to peace. Let peace fill our hearts, our world, our universe.

20

Prudence

Correct knowledge and good judgment
so one can choose and act for the good

Prudence might be thought of as an old-fashioned reality. Yet it is one of the four cardinal virtues and key to a faith-filled life: "Prudence is the virtue that disposes practical reason (the mind thinking about what should be done) to discern our true good in every circumstance and to choose the right means of achieving it" (*Catechism of the Catholic Church*, 1806).

Prudence has three steps: seeking the most loving thing to do (often with advice from others), judging what is the best choice, and confidently acting. Prudence goes beyond a human tendency (in today's busy world) to make decisions quickly and often based on what "feels" right.

APPROACHES

- Through continual and constant conversations, help your learners realize that prudence touches all areas of our lives—use of technology, simplicity/consumerism, decisions regarding actions, and much more.

- Walk with your learners as they realize that there is a difference between things that are permitted and things that are wise. Help them to learn how to count the possible costs of their decisions.

ACTIVITIES

- Invite your learners to research some people in Scripture who lived by the virtue of prudence (e.g., Queen Esther, St. Paul in his dealing with other cultures).

- Help your learners explore the three steps of prudence—seek, judge, and act—by suggesting everyday scenarios from their lives. How would they seek the most loving thing? What would help them to judge what is best? What might their action(s) be?

- Have your learners read a book about a saint and report to the group how this person models the virtue of prudence. Examples: St. Ignatius of Loyola, St. Benedict, St. Charles Borromeo.

- Create a recipe for prudent living. What ingredients do you need?

- Design a bumper sticker that would help someone understand the meaning of prudence.

- Take time at the end of each day (or once a week) to look back over decisions/actions with your children. Were these decisions/actions prudent? Why or why not? What made them prudent or imprudent? If they were imprudent, what could have preceded the decision/action?

- Discuss television programs that you watch where the virtue of prudence is practiced. Discuss how specific programs portray characters who practice poor judgment.

- Use a saint-of-the day calendar on your dinner table. Read about the saint, and think about how he or she lived prudently.

PRAYER

Gracious God, in every step of Jesus' life he was guided by the Holy Spirit, guided to prudent decisions and actions. Holy Spirit, steer me, with your gift of prudence, to choose and act always for the good.

21

Respect

How we feel about others (attitude of reverence or regard) and how we treat others (showing we care about their feelings and well-being)

All lives "are masterpieces of God's creation...and deserving of the utmost reverence and respect" (Pope Francis, July 28, 2013). The best way to teach respect is to show respect. There are also ways to "teach" this critical value all day long. Forming children (and ourselves) in this virtue also conveys crucial lessons in kindness, consideration, honesty, open-mindedness, and gratitude.

APPROACHES

- Instill a respect for differences among people. Learn about—and write to—people in different countries, learning about their culture, their gifts, and their challenges. Likewise, involve youngsters in activities to help them know their community. Find some common cause that will bring learners and the community together.

- Express shock at any racist or unkind remark or joke; encourage a conversation about the way disciples of Jesus would speak.

- Ask your learners to interview three people (different ages), asking their ideas on one way to show respect to others.

- Invite children to role-play respectful ways: when answering the phone, when talking with someone with whom they disagree, when invited to a friend's home for dinner, etc.

- Suggest a campaign poster about respect. Include the word "Respect" and two reasons why someone would want to vote for having respect at home, in school, in the neighborhood, etc.

- Have children use glue to write on bright-colored paper a few statements that respectful people might say to others. Sprinkle the letters with glitter.

- Invite students to research cyberbullying, designing an anti-cyberbullying sign campaign. Ask their schools if these signs could be displayed.

- Read about John Muir, Rachel Carson, or Jane Goodall. Discuss how they showed respect for the environment.

SUGGESTIONS FOR FAMILIES

- Watch a TV show together. Who was respectful or disrespectful? How? What did they do (not do)? Too many shows today get their laughs by making fun of parents (and others in authority) by making them look foolish. Help your children to talk about the lack of respect.

- Help your children to treat belongings with respect:

Help them to understand what gives something its worth. If your child tends to walk across the neighbor's grass, don't just correct them; mention all the time that the neighbors spend taking care of their lawn.

- Think less is more. When children have lots of things, they tend to have less appreciation for each item. Offer fewer toys, choosing ones they can use in a variety of creative ways.

PRAYER

God of life, we remember the sacredness of all your people. Created sacred and holy, we are made in your image and likeness. May we always recognize the dignity and worth of every person. Give us eyes to see your image so that respect for everyone and all creation becomes our way of life. Amen.

22

Responsibility

Responding to a duty or task that is required or expected

Responsibility is much more than completing a task. It's also about an attitude; the reality that, because of the dignity of each human person, each is called to participate and respond for the sake of the common good. Responsibility is inclusive: "In the end, everything has been entrusted to our protection, and all of us are responsible for it. Be protectors of God's gifts!" (Pope Francis, homily at his installation, March 19, 2013).

APPROACHES

- Most schools in Japan, China, and Russia do not employ custodians. They believe that requiring students to clean the school themselves teaches respect and responsibility and emphasizes equality. What can we do to call our children/youth to responsibility?

- Encourage group work and projects in which each learner has a different role to play. Have a debriefing session, leading them to see that unless each person takes responsibility, the product can't be finished.

- Discuss issues of responsibility with the children. Don't assume they know. Help them to reflect on their actions and the consequences.

- Invite a reflection on what comes first—rights or responsibilities. Do responsibilities need to be met before rights can be exercised? Do people have responsibilities toward each other?

- The principle of responsibility is recognized on nearly every page of the Bible. Here are just a few examples: Matthew 23:16; 27:24; 28:14; Luke 12:42; Acts 5:28; 19:40; Romans 14:4.

- Invite children/youth to write letters to themselves, describing various choices they can make to be responsible in many areas of their lives during the next six months. Have them place their letter in a self-addressed envelope, seal it, and give it to you. Mail them their letters in six months.

- Always expand the reality of responsibility to their role in a wider community. For example, remind them that we share responsibility for the planet: How can we reuse and recycle things?

SUGGESTIONS FOR FAMILIES

- Have family discussions about major family decisions. Ask: If we make this decision, what will be each person's responsibility?

- Be careful about taking away responsibility (e.g., delivering forgotten lunches, homework, books, etc.). Let children experience what happens naturally if they are not responsible.

- Give continual opportunities for responsibility (making their own lunch, organizing their bedroom, etc.). Encourage youth to do volunteer work—providing them with experiences where they need to be on time and to be pleasant, despite how they might be feeling, etc.

- Help your children make amends. Brainstorm ways to take responsibility—replacing a broken toy, inviting an excluded classmate to a party, etc.

PRAYER

Lord, take me where you want me to go; let me meet who you want me to meet; tell me what you want me to say, and keep me out of your way. (Fr. Mychal Judge, OFM)

23

Simplicity

Something that is ordinary, but enjoyable; the quality of being plain or not fancy, pretentious, complicated, or luxurious

REFLECTION FOR CATECHISTS

Simple living touches all aspects of life, strongly affecting our discipleship and spirituality. People living simply are clear and transparent; their relationships are honest and solid. The simple person is sincere with nothing to hide. God comes to us in simplicity: "The Lord is revealed in simplicity...It would do us good... to consider how the Lord has helped us in our lives...We will find that the Lord has always done this with simple things...The Lord does things simply" (Pope Francis, September 2015).

APPROACHES

- Connect experiences of "wanting more" to an awareness of others. Do our excesses, our comfort, etc., impact the poor?

- Simplify life by doing one thing at a time. Multitasking may be popular, but Scripture—and our experience—remind us of the benefits of being mindful, paying attention to the present moment (Ecclesiastes 3:1–8).Model mindfulness in all you do within your catechetical setting.

- Explore with youth their meeting places: the library, a park, a friend's house, the parish. Discuss: What does it mean when the preferred place to meet with friends is the mall, a place for buying and consuming?

- Explore commercials with children/youth. Help them be aware of strategies that are used to make us want to buy products. For example, ask: Do you think those shoes really helped him to get the basketball in the hoop—or has the star wearing them spent a lifetime practicing?

- Books to inspire simplicity and generosity: *The Quiltmaker's Gift*, *Too Many Toys*, *The Gift of Nothing*, *Little Bird*, and *Stuff*.

- Emphasize making gifts or presents of time and talent rather than buying more stuff.

SUGGESTIONS FOR FAMILIES

- Help everyone unclutter their schedule to have time for God, family, and giving to others. Rather than having many scheduled activities each week, enjoy hobbies, reading, and simply being.

- Avoid using gifts as a reward. While occasional treats for special occasions are appropriate, don't lead children into thinking that they deserve a present every time they do something that is asked of them. Celebrate with an extra trip to the playground or having a friend over to play.

- Slow down talk about material things—"We really need a new couch before we have company"; "That new shirt will make you look really cute." When children hear frequent comments about how we need material things, how they define us or make us look a certain way, it can send the wrong message.

God of simplicity, help me unclutter my many things, my packed schedule, and my busy mind so I can recognize you in all things, so I can be generous in my giving.

24

Trustworthiness

Being reliable and loyal; keeping promises; doing the right thing

Trustworthiness includes four major virtues: integrity (walking the talk), honesty (what we say and what we do), reliability (keeping promises and following through) and loyalty (standing up with and for someone in need). "Trustworthy persons are those who honor their commitments with seriousness and responsibility when they are being observed, but above all when they are alone; they radiate a sense of tranquility because they never betray a trust" (Pope Francis, December 21, 2015).

APPROACHES

- Whenever real-life situations arise in your group, talk about the concept of "cause and effect." "If a person is trustworthy, then..."

- Throughout the year, share and discuss various quotes about truthfulness, e.g., "When in doubt tell the truth" (Mark Twain); "The truth is not always the same as the majority decision" (St. John Paul II); "Whoever can be trusted with very little can also be trusted with much" (Luke 16:10a).

- Make a wheel with the word "trustworthy" as the hub. Choose words for the spokes that describe trustworthiness.

- You have just made the cover of Terrific Trust magazine. Draw yourself on that cover and list "articles" that indicate in words or pictures some of the stories included in that issue. For instance: "When My Parents Trust Me Most," "Five Times I've Been Trustworthy with My Friends," and "I Think Trust Is Really Important Because..."

- Trustworthiness includes all areas of our lives: family, friends, our many communities, God. Invite learners to brainstorm a list of the traits that make them trustworthy. Have learners work in small groups to write a cheer, chant, song, or poem that expresses their loyalty to God, their family, and/or their friends.

- Invite learners to interview adults in their life. Ask the adults to explain different situations in which trustworthiness proved to be invaluable.

- Have your group create a web of people that they can trust at school, at home, and in the community.

- As a family, watch for examples of trustworthiness: in each other, in your friends, and on TV shows and in movies. In what ways are these people trustworthy? In what ways would these relationships be different if they found you had not been trustworthy?

- Talk together—making a list for your refrigerator of ways to be trustworthy: Tell the truth. Keep your word. Be reliable. Return things you borrow. Keep private information private. Don't gossip. Don't ask a friend to do something wrong to keep your friendship. Stand up for, and act on, what you believe. Do the right thing, no matter what you lose in the process.

PRAYER

God who can always be trusted, help me to be like Jesus: a person of integrity, honesty, reliability, and loyalty.

25

Wonder

Rapt attention or astonishment at something awesomely mysterious or new to one's experience; the feeling aroused by something awe-inspiring, astounding, or marvelous

REFLECTION FOR CATECHISTS

As a gift of the Holy Spirit, wonder and awe helps us remember that God is creator and we are creatures. The sense of wonder leads us to admire each marvel, each grace, each surprise. We appreciate the extraordinary and the unique; we notice the little and great amazements of life. Wonder is the foundation for prayer and spills over into how we live: "Let the joyous wonder of Easter Sunday radiate through our thoughts, looks, attitudes, gestures and words" (Pope Francis, April 21, 2014).

APPROACHES

* Ask questions that prompt children to notice amazing details: "Listen! I hear something. What do *you* hear?" Or: "I see _____. Can you find it? What else can you find that is tiny?"

* Do not keep your wonder to yourself when you notice something strikingly beautiful. Tell your children how

much you like what God makes. Say: "I love how the trees make shadows on the road," or "I am so glad God made flowers to have a smell, aren't you?" Talk about God as an artistic Creator and an involved Provider.

ACTIVITIES

- Using wondering questions that allow for creativity, invite the learners to place themselves in the situation, and allow for multiple answers. For example: "I wonder how Mary Magdalene felt when Jesus' body was not in the tomb. I wonder what it was like to hear, 'Jesus is alive!' I wonder how Mary felt when Jesus called her by name. I wonder what it felt like to tell others that Jesus is risen!"

- Invite a reflection on questions like the following: What if we named something "wonderful" and treated it that way? I wonder if being filled with wonder makes me heavier or lighter…

- Invite your learners to wonder about fundamental issues: How can we put an end to war? How can we make sure all people have food? How can we care for creation? What might need to happen so all people can have safe homes?

SUGGESTIONS FOR FAMILIES

- Wonder together. Go on walks and bike rides and long drives with the windows down. Teach the value of the scenic route. Gather treasures on your wanderings. Collect leaves and rocks and flowers.

- Wonder bonds families together with shared discoveries.

If you are learning together as a family, you always have something interesting to talk about, and that can help unify your family. Each month decide on something that you will learn and explore together.

PRAYER

God of wonder, you have gifted us with wonder; we are in awe of everything around us. As wonder brings us closer to you, help us to cherish all your gifts.

Family Resources Center
415 NE Monroe
Peoria, IL 61603 (309) 839-2287